Dear Chris,

Thank you for the interest in this project!

BLACK TSUNAMI
JAPAN 2011

James Whitlow Delano

FotoEvidence

Black Tsunami: Japan 2011 by James Whitlow Delano
Copyright © 2013 FotoEvidence. All rights reserved.
Photographs Copyright © 2013 James Whitlow Delano
Afterword: Copyright © 2013 Bill Emmett

Photo Editor: Svetlana Bachevanova
Text Editor: David Stuart
Book Design: Mark Weinberg

FotoEvidence Press, New York
178 Frost Street, Brooklyn, NY 11211
FotoEvidence.com

Printed in Istanbul at Ofset Yapimevi

First edition

ISBN 978-0-9834913-7-8

FotoEvidence is a platform for documentary photographers whose work focuses on social justice and human rights.

FORWORD

BLACK TSUNAMI: JAPAN 2011

The first thing forgotten, when confronted by disaster, are the raw moments. Maybe it is a built-in human defense mechanism to protect us. Without them, all the hard edges are able to soften and the knife-slicing survival instincts start to fade to extinction like most dreams do in the morning. This collection of photographs was a conscious effort to remember from where the people of Tohoku have emerged. It is seared into their DNA now but, already, even the tsunami survivors' memories have begun to blur over time. Recently, I have mined these memories before they inevitably evaporate. *Black Tsunami: Japan 2011* is a part of that process.

    Fearing the worst, with the Fukushima Daiichi nuclear power plant melting down, we loaded up a rented van with extra cans of gasoline, water and food. We crossed Honshu at 3:00 am to the far, Sea of Japan coast. Roads would be clear over there and a spine of volcanic mountains, we believed, would at least partially protect us from the cloud of radioactivity that transformed from a worst fear into reality that day. It was a time when the impossible just kept happening.

By the time we cut back toward the Pacific side of Honshu, the rain had turned to snow. Supply lines were breaking down. Gas lines for cars extended for mile upon snowy mile, drivers could be seen huddling against the cold inside. Hours after dark, drivers would leave their cars in line overnight, returning to them again before dawn. I saw one man finally reach the front of a long gas line only to be told all the gas was gone. The man bowed graciously and returned to his car without saying a word: only in Japan.

We abandoned the van to hire a propane-fueled taxi to navigate the tsunami zone, because propane was plentiful.

We expected police to cordon off the tsunami disaster zone but they simply waved us through. The snow intensified as we entered the zone. I remember wanting to climb out the taxi window to photograph this otherworldly winter wonderland turned on its head.

Cars were folded like soft drink cans over bridge railings 15 meters above the water, trees were impaled through 3rd floor windows and boats were deposited on rooftops.

Survivors shuffled through the mud and snow in a state of shock. Soon we joined these shuffling masses, feet soaked with freezing cold black mud carried in by the tsunami. Moving inside provided little relief because inside evacuation centers temperatures hovered below 10° C (50° F) conditions that leaned heaviest on the very young and the very old. Removing our shoes, we entered in wet socks and flimsy plastic slippers. The survivors gathered in small family groups on blankets, striving to regain a modicum of privacy in a twilight pall of anemic lighting underpowered by gas-fueled generators with fuel in short supply. No words were necessary for communication. It was there I first encountered a peculiar 'infinity-stare,' born of worry, cold, hunger and lack of sleep. It would become a familiar expression in the time ahead.

Soon, though, the crisis at Fukushima Daiichi began to eclipse the tsunami disaster further north. At first, I wanted nothing to do with carcinogenic radiation. Soon, we learned new vocabulary like, "hibaku", "radiation" in Japanese, micro and milli-sieverts: how many x-rays worth of radiation we would be absorbing after hopping over barriers and evading police to photograph inside the nuclear no-entry zone.

The first time in it was Easter Sunday. The sun, brilliant in a cloudless sky, foretold the approach of spring as I skulked through a plantation forest of Japanese cypress, all the while being pelted by unseen, unfelt subatomic particles. My mind could not accept that all this lush, spring life was somehow contaminated. Descending through tall bamboo, I slipped into a farm compound where the family left so quickly that they did not have time to take the laundry off the line. Six weeks after the disaster it still flapped in the wind. I returned six months later and finally, again, one year later, as the now-soiled clothes still hung in tatters from the line.

Suddenly the government tells residents that they can return to their homes, but not live in them, in much of the former no-entry zone. Meanwhile, Geiger counter in hand, one and a half years after the meltdown, I stood outside the no-entry zone but directly downwind from Fukushima Daiichi, surrounded by bucolic perfection, that just happened to be a radiation hot spot that was capable of delivering a yearly dose of radiation in less than 24 hours. This is what the government has described as a safe place to return during the day. It is going to take a lot more than words to put Fukushima right again.

One year after the tsunami, on March 11, 2012, a family gathered at an empty lot where their house once stood in Ishinomaki, Miyagi Prefecture. One of them was holding a little Buddhist monument dedicated to a lost family member. As I approached to photograph them I remember feeling uncomfortable intruding and thinking, "I don't want to do this" but I knew I had to. Our eyes met and smiles broke out. They handed me a couple of digital cameras so that I could take photographs for *them*. They even asked me to stand among them to be photographed together. We parted laughing. We all laughed together that day, exactly one year after the Black Tsunami had changed all our lives forever.

PART ONE

On March 11, 2011, the Tohoku earthquake, measuring 9.0 on the Richter scale rocked Japan. The quake, the fourth strongest ever recorded and the strongest ever to strike Japan, sent a tsunami that peaked at 39 meters (128 ft.) onto Japan's east coast. The quake and tsunami killed thousands of people, leveled entire towns and villages, and critically damaged nuclear reactors at the Fukushima Daiichi power station.

Japan counts 15,883 confirmed dead, 6,145 injured, and 2,671 people still missing.

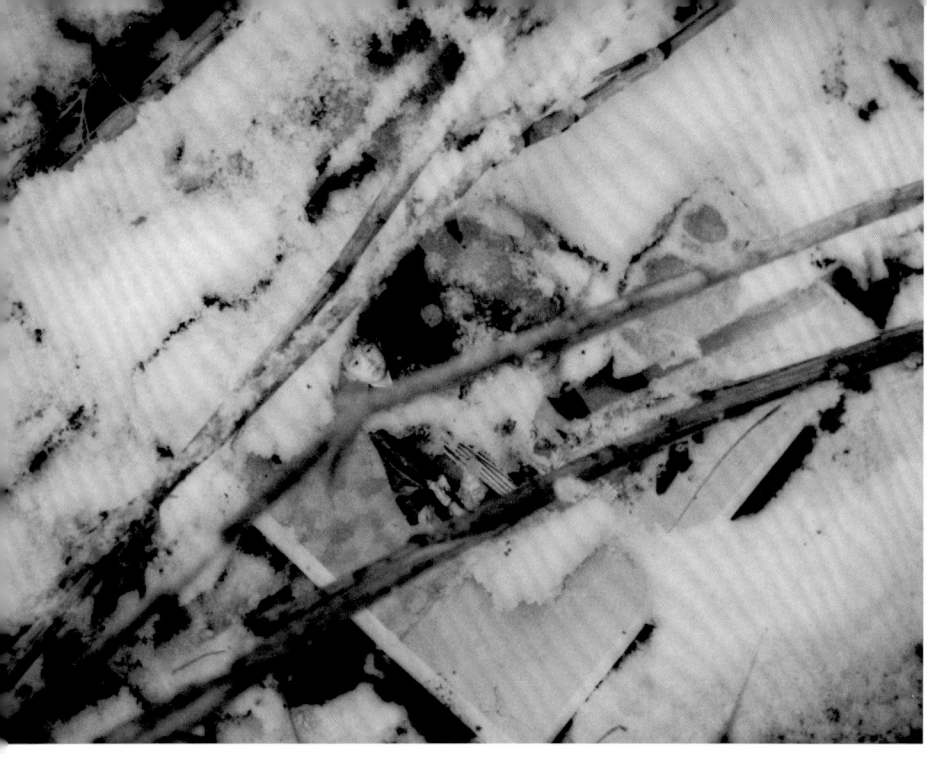

As a result of the earthquake and tsunami, over 400,000 people moved to evacuation centers in schools and public buildings. One million and four hundred thousand people were without running water and 2.5 million households were left without heat and electricity.

Forty-six thousand buildings were destroyed and another 144,000 were damaged. An estimated 230,000 cars and trucks were destroyed. The tsunami littered the landscape with 25 million tons of debris.

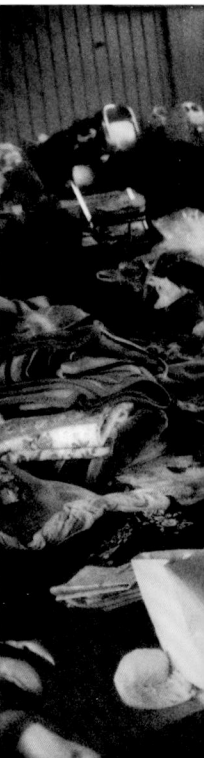

PART TWO

The damage to the Fukushima Daiichi nuclear reactors led to radiation releases and the evacuation of 88,000 people that lived within 20 km (12.4 miles) of the damaged reactors.

The most contaminated areas still remain closed, those residents living in temporary units spread out all over Fukushima Prefecture and further. The Japanese government pulled back the nuclear no-entry to within 10 km (6.2 miles) of the crippled nuclear plant in April 2012, and pulled it back again in April 2013 to within 5km (3.1 miles), where residents may visit but not live. As of May 27, 2013, the last remaining town of Futaba was opened to residents, though overnight stays will not be permitted.

Throughout Japan, people still fear radioactive contamination from rice and livestock that may have been exposed to nuclear fallout or that is currently cultivated on the edge of the exclusion zone. Farmers in the fallout zone have begun decontaminating their fields but many consumers are reluctant to buy their products, even with assurances of food safety from the farmers and government?

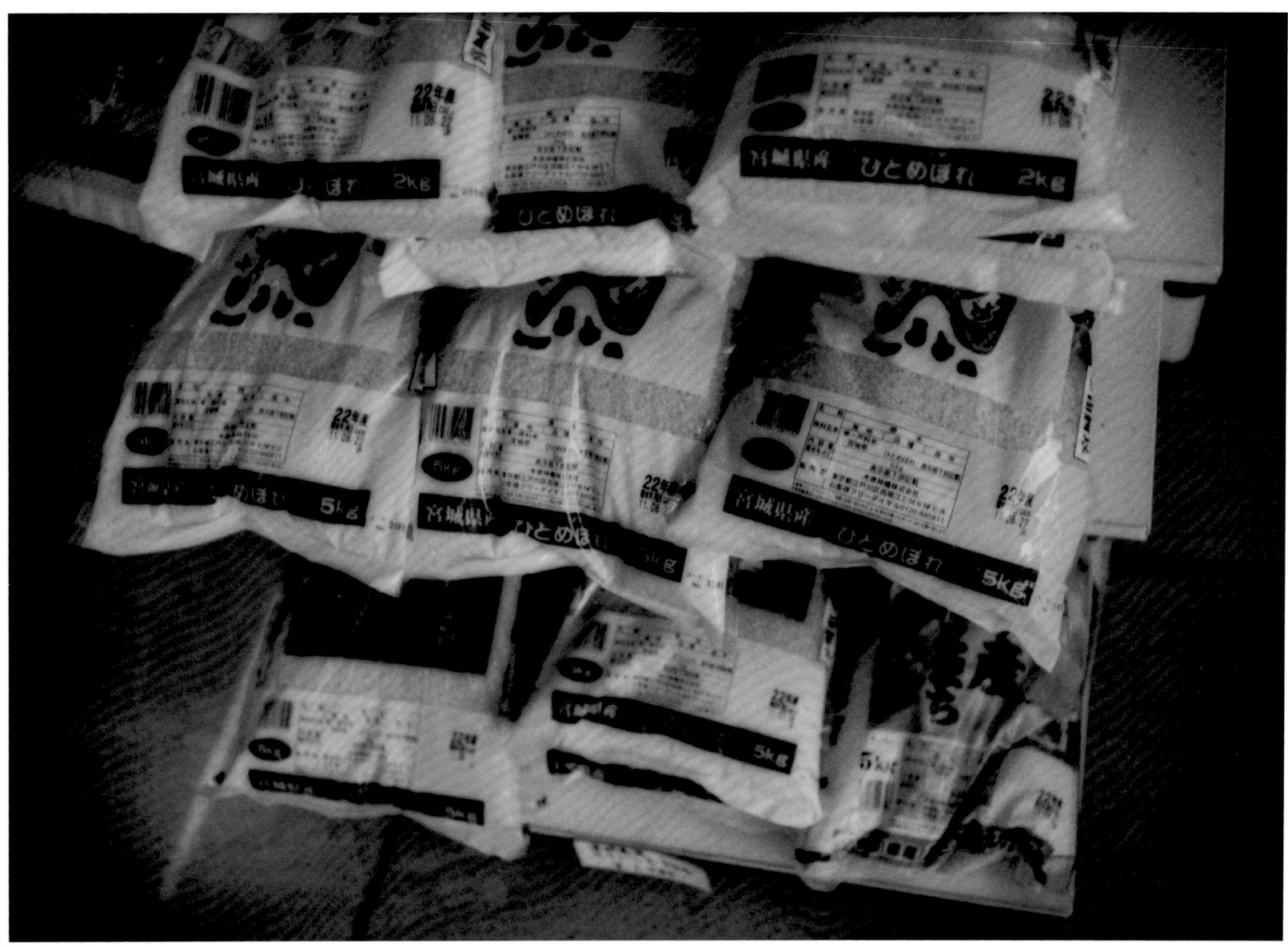

PART THREE

The Black Tsunami has left an indelible mark on Japan. Analysts estimate direct damage at between $290 and $350 Billion, making it the most costly natural disaster ever. Indirect costs to the economy are estimated at an additional $200 to $300 Billion.

The northeastern part of the country faces years of rebuilding despite a massive clean up effort. Much of the recovery effort in the tsunami disaster zone has stalled for many reasons, including bureaucratic inertia and inability of communities to raise funds. Many residents' have been forbidden to rebuild on land deemed too vulnerable to a future tsunami. So, hundreds of kilometers of the Tohoku coast is scattered with ghost towns, where many residents have chosen to pick up their lives and move elsewhere.

Cleaning up the contaminated Fukushima Daiichi power station is estimated to take 40 years. The meltdown at the Fukushima Daiichi reactors shook confidence in the safety of nuclear power, on which Japan depends for almost a third of its electricity. Long-standing plans for the expansion of nuclear power are being called into question. The effects of the Black Tsunami will be felt for years to come.

PART FOUR

AFTERWORD

The Black Tsunami was one of the most widely witnessed—perhaps the most widely witnessed—natural disasters in history, thanks to the ubiquity of video cameras and mobile phones. So in some sense we all, all over the world, felt a greater affinity with the people of Tohoku than is the case with conventional earthquakes, for example, where the deadly event is over quickly and is invisible to most of us, apart from the ensuring destruction.

So it might follow logically that having watched the horrific events of March 11th on television, there would be no need to go to the region personally, even if, like me, you have been following Japan as a journalist for nearly 30 years. It might, but that would be wrong. I felt an irresistible pull, tugging me not just from my home in England to Japan, but to the Tohoku coast itself, three weeks after the tsunami and the Fukushima Dai-Ichi nuclear accident.

For there is something crucial that videos on television miss. That something is the humanity, the human consequences of a disaster of this sort. Going to the region did, admittedly, also provide a clearer sense of the sheer scale of what had happened, destruction far more complete and powerful than in any war zone bar Hiroshima in 1945, a destruction with an extraordinary feeling of contrast between one street that had been spared and another, a few unlucky steps away, that simply no longer existed.

But more than anything, it was the people that I learned from, the people that stick still now in my memory. The waitress in a Sendai restaurant, clad in a bright kimono, fighting back the tears as she told of the family members she had lost. The elderly man, directing traffic at the hospital car park in Onagawa, who points to a black car perched on the top of a distant five-storey building, saying it was his and it was parked in that very car park. The smartly dressed taxi-driver, white gloves and all, who took me to see the tsunami damage in Sendai's port, and said he was living in an evacuation centre as his house had been swept away.

The same feeling, of March 11th as above all a human tragedy, came when I returned to the same towns six months later to see how much had changed. Debris had been cleared, the signs of mud had more or less gone, and a few scraps of rebuilding had begun. But the over-riding sense was of emptiness and depression, a feeling of hopelessness in the face of the scale of the task of reconstruction—and, I naturally wondered, in the face of the incoherence and sheer dysfunctionality of the political response. This time it was the sight of a lonely man, standing on the port of Onagawa and just staring silently out to sea that sticks in my memory.

An outsider's memory is of little importance compared with the memories of the people of Tohoku, and of the rest of Japan, for they will not forget March 11th for centuries, if ever. But it is nevertheless important to share those Japanese memories, in however small a way, to maintain a sense of solidarity, of understanding, and above all of our human vulnerability in the face of nature's force.

Bill Emmott
MARCH 2012

CAPTIONS

Page 3
An ocean going ship sits where it came to rest in the debris of the great tsunami that hit Kesennuma, Miyagi Prefecture following the massive Tohoku earthquake that struck off the coast of Japan.

Page 4
Six months after one of the biggest tsunamis in recorded history ravaged this coast, and triggered the world's second biggest nuclear power plant crisis, the ocean washes placidly on the Fukushima Prefecture shoreline. KOBAMA, FUKUSHIMA PREFECTURE.

Page 9
Flotsam from a town completely flattened by the tsunami. RIKUZEN-TAKATA, IWATE PREFECTURE.

Page 10
An elderly woman shuffles through a city wiped off the face of the earth by the tsunami that arrived 30 minutes after the largest earthquake in Japan's recorded history. RIKUZEN-TAKATA, IWATE PREFECTURE. In Rikuzen-Takata 10,547 residents, nearly half the population, are living in evacuation shelters. About 5,000 of the city's houses were submerged by the quake-triggered tsunami.

Page 12
The formidable sea wall, still standing at the right of the image, was not enough to halt the black wave that hit this village, TONI, IWATE PREFECTURE. Residents here claim that the tsunami was 30 m (almost 100 ft) high. Houses on the hill (in the top left) were damaged up to the second floor.

Page 15
Japan Self Defense Forces search several kilometers inland from Otsuchi for victims of the tsunami. Clothing and a sofa from a demolished house are suspended from the branches of a tree. The cold weather that set in right after the tsunami hampered the relief effort and weighed heavily on the elderly and young children.
IWATE PREFECTURE.

Page 13
Rescue workers pause from work for a collective prayer for the dead, a week after the precise moment the tsunami struck Ofunato, IWATE PREFECTURE.

Page 16
Tsunami survivors from Otsuchi line up for dinner at an evacuation center in a middle school, where 700 people whose houses have been damaged or destroyed live. Food and fresh water were in short supply as all the shops in the town were flattened and supplies were only trickling through due to the fuel shortage.
OTSUCHI, IWATE PREFECTURE.

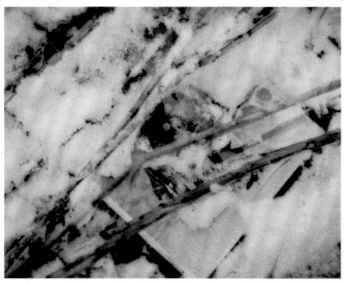

Page 14 LEFT
Portrait of a young boy found several kilometers inland from the sea, swept there by the tsunami, where it was exposed in the snow. The fate of the young boy in the photograph is unknown. OTSUCHI, IWATE PREFECTURE.

Page 18 LEFT
A father brushes his daughter's teeth at an unheated evacuation center for survivors of the tsunami. There is no running water at the middle school which serves as an evacuation center, so water must be used sparingly.
OTSUCHI, IWATE PREFECTURE.

Page 14 RIGHT
Navigating the road to Otsuchi past a house that was swept up and deposited on the side of the road.
IWATE PREFECTURE.

Page 18 RIGHT
Seniors huddle near a kerosene heater to ward of the ever-present cold stalking tsunami survivors at an evacuation. Kerosene was in short supply and electricity was supplied by gas powered generators until the electric power grid could be repaired.
OTSUCHI, IWATE PREFECTURE.

Page 19
Ofunato resident, standing upon the rubble of his house, talks with rescue worker. Throughout the region, families could be seen rummaging through the remains of their homes, looking for mementos and family valuables. IWATE PREFECTURE.

Page 22 RIGHT
A rescue worker stands guard over the body of a victim, a man in his 50's, that a rescue crew from Taiwan had located buried in the rubble of OFUNATO, IWATE PREFECTURE.

Page 20
A tug boat has been deposited high above the harbor, which is more than 1 kilometer away, behind a house that may not have originally stood in that location. The branches of the cherry trees are strewn with clothing and refuse at a second storey level. OFUNATO, IWATE PREFECTURE.

Page 23
A main road flooded by the quake-triggered tsunami with buildings whose original locations were likely not where they rest now. KESENNUMA, MIYAGI PREFECTURE.

Page 21
A car deposited on the rail of high bridge submerged in the tsunami waters at KAMAISHI, IWATE PREFECTURE. The building in the background, despite being atop an embankment, had tsunami waters reach the second storey.

Page 24
An elderly woman searches for food to buy among empty shelves in a convenience store. After the tsunami, the most important supply routes north were closed and impassable to trucks carrying cargo. Bottled water, gasoline, kerosene and food became scarce in the tsunami zone. KITAKAMI, IWATE PREFECTURE.

Page 22 LEFT
A charred debris field is all that remains of central Kesennuma, which caught fire after the tsunami leveled the city. MIYAGI, PREFECTURE.

Page 25
Double lines for fuel. People have lined up for kerosene (toyu) because it is common to have portable kerosene heaters in Japan, where central heating is almost non-existent. OFUNATO, IWATE PREFECTURE. Gasoline was in such short supply that most gas stations were closed and those that opened limited customers to 20 liters (5.4 gallons) of gasoline after waiting in long lines. Lines were so long that some people parked cars in line overnight and went home until the station opened again in the morning.

Page 26
There was no escape. A resident of Rikuzen-Takata walks at the high water mark of the great tsunami several kilometers from the sea and still lumber is piled up on rooftops. The rest of the city was completely leveled. RIKUZEN-TAKATA, IWATE PREFECTURE.

Page 32 LEFT
Seats on a bus used to transport workers to the stricken Fukushima Daiichi Nuclear Power Plant in May 2011 are wrapped in special white fabric so that radioactive material will have a difficult time penetrating the seats and carpet of the interior. HIRONOMACHI, FUKUSHIMA PREFECTURE.

Page 27
Fish were scattered when the March 11 tsunami ripped through several fish processing plants in Ofunato. They remain where they came to rest more than one month before but now petals of cherry blossoms have fallen onto the fish as each return to the soil, OFUNATO, IWATE PREFECTURE.

Page 32 RIGHT
A nuclear power plant worker pauses before boarding one of the charter buses bound for the stricken Fukushima Daiichi Nuclear Power Plant at the off-limits J Village, after the photographer managed to enter the facility in May 2011. HIRONOMACHI, FUKUSHIMA PREFECTURE.

Page 29
A Somei-Yoshino cherry tree, the symbol of rebirth in Japanese culture, has survived the devastating tsunami and blossomed as spring returns to the Tohoku region of Japan. OFUNATO, IWATE PREFECTURE.

Page 33
Recovery workers wearing full-body, white hazardous materials (hazmat) suits to protect them from radiation, enter what was the 20 km (12.4 miles) nuclear no-entry zone in a police bus at the main check point on Route 6 in April 2011. MINAMI SOMA, FUKUSHIMA PREFECTURE. The no-entry zone has recently been all but eliminated.

Page 30
Police from Tokyo man the main check point on Route 6 in early April 2011 on the southern side of the nuclear no-entry zone in front of J Village, originally built as a national training facility for young Japanese football (soccer) players, but is now used as a staging facility for workers to don radiation protection suits for work at the Fukushima Daiichi Nuclear Power Plant. HIRONOMACHI, FUKUSHIMA PREFECTURE.

Page 34
Route 6 completely failed and crumbled away during the earthquake at the main southern police checkpoint for the nuclear no-entry zone. HIRONOMACHI, FUKUSHIMA PREFECTURE.

Page 35
Salt left on a rice field inundated by sea water, which soaked millions of hectares (2.47 acres) along the coast of Japan's Tohoku region. FUKUSHIMA PREFECTURE.

Page 38 RIGHT
The central shopping district is shuttered in the veritable ghost town of Kawauchi Village in May 2011, FUKUSHIMA PREFECTURE.

Page 36
Two images of the same hanging clothes drying rack. Here, clothes hang six weeks after the government enforced evacuation inside the nuclear no-entry zone.

Page 39
A cow and her unseen calf housed in a barn right in front of a barrier to the Fukushima nuclear no-entry zone in January 2012, on the border of territory too contaminated for human habitation. Cattle were still raised here and their milk may be sold. as long as their feed comes from outside the region. The entire area is surrounded by land contaminated with radioactive cesium. On August 25, 2011, the Japanese government lifted a ban on shipping beef from Fukushima Prefecture. IWAKIOTA, FUKUSHIMA PREFECTURE.

Page 37
Here, the laundry hangs in tatters 6 months later. Near ODAKA, FUKUSHIMA PREFECTURE. In April 2012, the government lifted the ban on entry to the town where this house sits but residents can only visit and may not stay overnight.

Page 40
Looking out over salt-fouled rice fields where concrete tetra-pods are piled up along the beach. They have been picked up and left stranded several hundred meters inland. This land has subsided nearly 1 meter (3.28 ft), meaning it may no longer be arable because of high tides. MINAMI SOMA, FUKUSHIMA PREFECTURE.

Page 38 LEFT
A heavy police presence in the veritable ghost town of Kawauchi Village in May 2011, which straddled the line of the 20 km nuclear no-entry zone in force at the time. Originally, half of the village was within the exclusion zone but the police check point was moved back to the edge of the village. It still sat within the 30 km (18.6 miles) voluntary evacuation zone where residents were encouraged to stay indoors and be ready for immediate evacuation if necessary. Some villagers were beginning to return but the village remained a ghost town. FUKUSHIMA PREFECTURE.

Page 41
Grave monuments left toppled and embedded in mud by the tsunami inside the nuclear no-entry zone. OSAKU, NEAR ODAKA, FUKUSHIMA PREFECTURE. One of the most cited concerns of evacuees is their inability to tend to their ancestors' graves.

Page 42 LEFT
Looking through a door ajar into a house, in April 2011, ransacked after its family was ordered to leave because of fears of radiation from the Fukushima Daiichi Nuclear Power Plant. Near ODAKA, FUKUSHIMA PREFECTURE. In April 2012, the government lifted the ban on entry to the town where this house sits but residents can only visit and may not stay overnight.

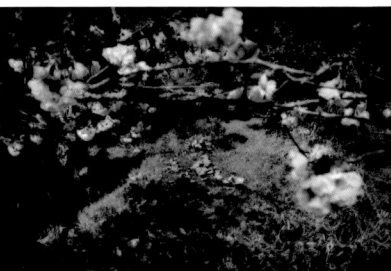

Page 45 LEFT
Yae-zakura (eight-pedal cherry blossoms), still associated with the ancient capital Nara, bloom in the garden behind an evacuated farm house in April 2011 inside the nuclear no-entry zone, as spring returns.
OGISAKU, NEAR ODAKA, FUKUSHIMA PREFECTURE.

Page 42 RIGHT
What looks like a farmer's favorite chair sits with boots hastily throw beneath it at an evacuated farmhouse in April 2011 in the nuclear no-entry zone. Near ODAKA, FUKUSHIMA PREFECTURE.

Page 45 RIGHT
Potted plants wither and die on the doorstep of a farmhouse inside the nuclear no-entry zone in April 2011. NEAR OKUBOMAE, NEAR ODAKA, FUKUSHIMA PREFECTURE. In April 2012, the government lifted the ban on entry to the town where this house sits but residents can only visit and may not stay overnight.

Page 43
This tranquil patch of forest lies within the no-entry zone and provided cover to move around on this Sunday morning in April 2011. Near ODAKA, FUKUSHIMA PREFECTURE. The Japanese government declared the no-entry zone off-limits under the Disaster Countermeasures Basic Law which gives the police the power to detain anyone entering the zone for up to 30 days and impose a fine of up 100,000 JPY (US $1,200), a risk the photographer took to make this photograph.

Page 47
A cherry tree that survived the tsunami and sprouted blossoms, despite debris dangling from its branches, OFUNATO, IWATE PREFECTURE.

Page 44
Weeds begin to overrun a greenhouse, in April 2011, inside the nuclear no-entry zone at an evacuated farm, near ODAKA, FUKUSHIMA PREFECTURE.

Page 48 LEFT
Soybeans cultivated inside the nuclear exclusion zone, behind barriers forbidding entry, in an area where rice cultivation is forbidden. IWAKIOTA, FUKUSHIMA PREFECTURE.

Page 48 RIGHT
A barrier, marking the 20 km nuclear no-entry zone, overgrown with vines six months after the crisis began. NEAR MINAMI SOMA, FUKUSHIMA PREFECTURE.

Page 51
Tracks inside the nuclear exclusion zone leading south toward the crippled Fukushima Dai Ichi Nuclear power Plant, six months after the tsunami struck.

Page 49
A planted flower garden ends precisely at the barriers barring entry into the nuclear no-entry zone. MEMEZAWA, FUKUSHIMA PREFECTURE.

Page 52
Farmland inside the nuclear no-entry zone which was not planted because of fears of radioactive iodides and cesium being absorbed into crops, six weeks after the nuclear meltdown.

Page 50 LEFT
Farmhouse, within the nuclear exclusion zone, six months after the forced evacuation, near ODAKA, FUKUSHIMA PREFECTURE.

Page 53
Weeds run wild in the same fields six months later, as the government conceded that vast areas inside the no-entry zone may remain unsafe for human habitation for decades. NEAR ODAKA, FUKUSHIMA PREFECTURE.

Page 50 RIGHT
Curtains are drawn closed at an uninhabited farm compound, where the garden has run wild, six months after the mandatory evacuation order came from the central government for all residents within 20 km (12.4 miles) of the Fukushima Daiichi Nuclear Power Plant. NEAR ODAKA, FUKUSHIMA PREFECTURE.

Page 54
Concrete tetra-pods that were swept hundreds of meters are brought back to the beach where they failed to stop the tsunami's onslaught. NEAR KOBAMA, FUKUSHIMA PREFECTURE.

Page 55
Concrete reminders of the tsunami, like this van inside the nuclear no-entry zone, are being overrun by salt resistant wild grass six months after the disaster. KOBAMA, FUKUSHIMA PREFECTURE.

Page 59
Six months after the disaster, the debris has been collected into piles and grass has begun to cover the scars caused by the tsunami. KOBAMA, NEAR ODAKA, FUKUSHIMA PREFECTURE.

Page 56
Rice for sale in a convenience store just outside the nuclear exclusion zone. None of it is from Fukushima Prefecture, which until the nuclear disaster was famous for growing some of the finest rice in Japan. The rice in this photograph is from neighboring Miyagi Prefecture. MINAMI SOMA, FUKUSHIMA PREFECTURE.

Page 60
Iwakiota Train Station straddles the nuclear no-entry zone line but no trains have arrived in the station since the tsunami hit and none are likely to arrive for a long time to come. IWAKIOTA, FUKUSHIMA PREFECTURE.

Page 57
A hand-painted sign protesting a proposal to dump radiation-contaminated tsunami debris up this road right on the nuclear no-entry zone line. NEAR KOBAMA, FUKUSHIMA PREFECTURE.

Page 61
Evidence of the tsunami and the debris it carried far and wide has been largely cleaned up. The remaining debris is beginning to be overgrown with vegetation. KAIBAMA, FUKUSHIMA PREFECTURE.

Page 58
Six weeks after the tsunami struck, debris and a concrete slab foundation are all that remain of a house where the tsunami thundered up a gap in cliffs.

Page 62 LEFT
Overgrown greenhouse inside the nuclear no-entry zone. NEAR ODAKA, FUKUSHIMA PREFECTURE.

Page 62 RIGHT
Six month ago, before this photograph was made and before the tsunami, this bucolic meadow was a community and rice paddies. A house foundation can be seen to the left, though salt resistant grass has run wild because the soil is too contaminated with salt and radioactive cesium for farmers to attempt to plant rice again. Just outside the nuclear exclusion zone, near KOBAMA, FUKUSHIMA PREFECTURE.

Page 68
Dump trucks wait in a long line to empty their tsunami rubble into the permanent dump site on an artificial peninsula of landfill in the port area of ISHINOMAKI, MIYAGI PREFECTURE. The disposal of millions of tons of debris containing but nuclear and non-nuclear contamination poses a challenge for the region and the country. The Environmental Ministry estimates that the tsunami dumped 22.7 million tons of debris in coastal Tohoku.

Page 63
A persistent concern among families forced to evacuate because of the Fukushima Daiichi meltdown was that they would be denied visitation to their families graves. Sunflowers have wilted at a grave a few hundred meters outside the exclusion zone. NEAR KAIBAMA, FUKUSHIMA PREFECTURE.

Page 69
Traditional tatami mat flooring from houses destroyed by the tsunami deposited at a permanent dump for tsunami debris. ISHINOMAKI, MIYAGI PREFECTURE.

Page 65
Two older women climb a hill that provided sanctuary from the mighty tsunami and the cherry trees, which were safe from the torrent, rooted in higher ground, blossom as spring returns to the tsunami zone. OFUNATO, IWATE PREFECTURE.

Page 70
A fisherman lost in thought gazing out toward a huge, temporary dump site that has risen across the Kitakami River from the main part of Ishinomaki in the tsunami zone, raising worries about air born asbestos and dioxins, and contamination of the ground and river water. MIYAGI PREFECTURE.

Page 66
The slow, steady clean up continues in front of a cherry tree which blossoms having survived the massive tsunami and avoiding a tug boat which was carried past it until it grounded. OFUNATO, IWATED PREFECTURE.

Page 71
A worker sprays disinfectant in a neighborhood near one of Ishinomaki's temporary dumps for tsunami debris to reduce the risk of disease from bacterial contaminated airborne dust. MIYAGI PREFECTURE.

Page 72 LEFT
A grandfather clock, that stopped at just about the time the tsunami struck dumped on a pile of personal belonging in a permanent dump. Debris has been separated into piles of concrete, wood, traditional tatami mats, clothes, paper, home furnishings, etc.
ISHINOMAKI, MIYAGI PREFECTURE.

Page 75
Instant Toxic Mountains: Toxic tsunami rubble has been piled up in front of an unoccupied apartment building were the tsunami swept through up to the third story.
ISHINOMAKI, MIYAGI PREFECTURE.

Page 72 RIGHT
Six months after the tsunami struck, this family tomb remains open, its urns containing ashes exposed to the elements. Many tombs in this cemetery have not been closed again. ISHINOMAKI, MIYAGI PREFECTURE.

Page 76 TOP
Lumber from houses destroyed by the tsunami is piled high at a permanent dump site where a crane can be seen spraying water because the wood has been catching fire from spontaneous combustion due to the heat and methane emitted during decomposition. The spontaneous combustion adversely affects the local air quality. YURIAGE, MIYAGI PREFECTURE.

Page 73
Sea water still sits in a former rice paddy that subsided below sea level, next to a permanent dump for the toxic tsunami rubble in Yuriage. MIYAGI PREFECTURE.

Page 76 BOTTOM
A repository for some of the hundreds of thousands of automobiles destroyed by the tsunami. Most of the cars that were destroyed were not covered by insurance and were a total loss for their owners.
ISHINOMAKI, MIYAGI PREFECTURE.

Page 74
The Shinto shrine which used to stand on top of the 6.2 meter high Hiyoriyama hillock, topped by a pine tree, was washed away by the tsunami. The mounds on each side were built with concrete rubble to park heavy machinery atop them every night in case another tsunami should strike. Eventually the concrete will be reused to raise land subsided during the earthquake and tsunami. YURIAGE, MIYAGI PREFECTURE.

Page 77
The last structure in what used to be a thriving residential community being dismantled before the materials are carted off to a tsunami debris dump nearby in the devastated community of Yuriage.
MIYAGI PREFECTURE.

Page 79
Cherry blossoms have opened on a tree that seems to rise right out of the rubble. OFUNATO, IWATE PREFECTURE.

Page 84 LEFT
A barrier barring entry into Iitate-mura village buried in snow. Iitate-mura is in the heart of the expanded nuclear evacuation zone because of high wind-driven radioactive fall-out from the Fukushima Daiichi nuclear power plant. and residents are not likely to return for years or maybe for decades. FUKUSHIMA PREFECTURE.

Page 80
Sea water bubbles up from below a street in the port district of Kesenuma. The district floods during every high tide because the Tohoku coast subsided almost 1 meter (3.28 feet) because of the earthquake and tsunami, MIYAGI PREFECTURE.

Page 84 RIGHT
A peaceful winter scene in the extended evacuation zone where not a soul has passed since the snow fell. Tsushima residents were forced to evacuate their village after a wind-driven radioactive cloud from the Fukushima Daiichi nuclear power plant scored a direct hit on this valley. Estimated annual radiation levels exceed 50 millisieverts, making the village uninhabitable for years or decades as Tsushima is one of most irradiated villages in Fukushima Prefecture.

Page 82
The massive tsunami wall at Toni that the tsunami pushed over. The neighborhood behind it was totally destroyed. IWATE PREFECTURE.

Page 85
Twilight on a lonely highway through the runs in the tsunami zone of OTSUCHI, IWATE PREFECTURE. Depopulation in the tsunami zone has become a great concern as families are choosing to pick up their lives and move elsewhere.

Page 83
An ocean going ship remains in place, blocking a street, one year after the tsunami in KESENUMA, MIYAGI PREFECTURE.

Page 86
Earthquake damage is still evident on the deserted main street of Odaka, which was inside the Fukushima nuclear no-entry zone until April 2012. Now the town is open for public access but residents are not permitted to live in the city because many districts lack running water and sewage. One store, a barber shop, is open on main street but there is nowhere to buy any food or supplies of any kind. Farming is not permitted. One of the biggest challenges will be to attract employers to return to the town, only a few have. ODAKA VILLAGE, MINAMI-SOMA, FUKUSHIMA PREFECTURE.

Page 87
A decontamination work crew on the main highway that links highly radioactive Iitate-mura with Fukushima City and the sea. Residents may return to Iitate-mura but the levels of radiation make it too dangerous to inhabit full time. That said, some residents have apparently returned and refused to leave. IITATE-MURA, FUKUSHIMA PREFECTURE.

Page 90 RIGHT
A farmer in hazmat suit and mask to protect him from radioactive fallout in the soil looks out over a field undergoing decontamination. Contaminated soil is packed into large sacks and stored under white tarpaulins. ON THE TOMIOKA HIGHWAY, BETWEEN TSUSHIMA AND YAMAKIYA, FUKUSHIMA PREFECTURE.

Page 88
Standing on a hot spot, in a garden in front of a Iitate-mura house, on a road that has already been decontaminated. Residents may return to their homes but cannot live in the village due to high levels of radiation. IITATE-MURA, FUKUSHIMA PREFECTURE.

Page 91
A farmer, wearing a hazmat suit to protect against high rates of radiation, cuts weeds that have taken over his field so that he can then plough under or remove the contaminated topsoil altogether so that radiation levels in future crops can meet Japanese national standards. IITATE-MURA, FUKUSHIMA PREFECTURE.

Page 89
An elderly man walks down a radiation-hot-spot-riddled street in Iitate-mura, where he lives, despite the fact that the Japanese government has designated the area as a radiation evacuation zone. It is legal to enter Iitate-mura but residents are not permitted to spend the night in the town. FUKUSHIMA PREFECTURE.

Page 92
Once a great pine forest of 70,000 trees covered the oceanfront at Takata Matsubara, until the tsunami swept through decimating them all. Now the sea under cuts the roots beneath their stumps, giving them an other worldly appearance. RIKUZEN-TAKATA, IWATE PREFECTURE.

Page 90 LEFT
Workers in hazmat protective clothing remove radiation contaminated topsoil from rice fields in Iitate-mura attempting to reduce the radioactivity to safe levels. The contaminated soil is being buried in shallow pits near by and then covered up. FUKUSHIMA PREFECTURE.

The publication of "Black Tsunami: Japan 2011" was made possible with the backing of the following people:

Jamie Irena Rayer Keet • Peter Sillem • Steven Nagelberg • Staton Winter • Karen Zusman • John McDermott • Sylvere Azoulai • Corinne Tapia • Marty Chumbes • John D. Upton • Angie Jennings • Akiko Arai • Eric Beecroft • Edwin Koo • John Stanmeyer • Dilla Djalil-Daniel • Clive France • Paul Lowe • Charlie Kirk • Daniel Berehulak • Sean Breslin • Mervyn Leong • Thomas Bregulla • Barbara Rachko • Robert Farley • Najat Naba • Kaz Kushida • Steven Koves • Bert Rothkugel • S. Katz • Nicholas Tay • Molly Rob • Ford Roosevelt • Matthew Goddard-Jones • Laurie Nalepa • Francois Tang • Palani Mohan • Will Baxter • Derek Schwartz • Eric John Kim • Kazunao Kubotera • Andrea Bonisoli Alquati • David Dare Parker Alejandro Cartagena • Thomas Haeussler Albi • Paige Mushinsky • Stephen Ferry • Mary Jesse • Tom Ashe • Michael Marten • Paolo Patrizi Tony McNicol • Makiko Hamada • Vincent Assante Di Cupillo • Richard Bram • Rob Yeichner • Kenneth Hughes • Thierry Hurzeler • Kevin Paul Ryan • Lourdes Jeannette • Hans Jürgen Balmes • Sally Clark • David Butow • Sølveig Bång • Auke Hulst • F.G. Fitz-Gerald • Allison Clark • Simon Keller • Jim Powell • David Barbour • John Goodyear • Steven Eckler • Susan Delsandro Hellier • Ayumi Nakanishi • Andrew Testa • Nina Berman • Sean Jensen • Treve Hodsman • Clifford Wright • Sara Terry • Michael Wong • Stella Kramer • Carolyn Beller • Michael Grecco • Adriana Zehbrauskas • Sylvain Demange • Rick Sanborn • Nina Sillem • Leslie Powell • Kevin J. Miyazaki • Coleen Jose • Mark Peterson • Stuart Isett • Brendan Casey • Christina Malkoun • Drue Zaharis • Bob Black • Lara Damiani • Bill Aron • Paul Giguere • Mario Zanot • Blair Farley • Stein Saugnes • Conor Risch • Sim Chiyin • Jack Harris • John Nelson • Bill Richmond • Jake Price • Michael Shaw • Derek Hudson • Stanka Usha Tsonkova • Jaime R. Carrero • Brenden Allen • Ray Simone • Andri Tambunan • Meryl Mohan • Stephen Paternite • John Yamartino • David Cicconi • Suzanne Kamata • Takaki Yajima • Kevin C. Downs • Tomoko Yamamoto • Shinichi ‹George› Hoshi • Christopher LaMarca and Katrina Taylor • Samson Yee • Andrew Chew • Matthieu Paley • Jeremy Sutton-Hibbert • The Ocean Net Works • Mary Jurek • Shiho Fukada • Camille Seaman • Yoonki Kim • David Jakle • Dave Haylett • Giorgio Baravalle • Andrew Darlow • Sandra Mau • Lori Grinker • Endo Tom Markey • Takashi Owaki • Gina Martin Adriana Roca • Ikaraam Ullah • Chris Taylor • Sam Middleton • Brian English • Aiko Matsumura • Toru Seno • Kevin Kato • Leslie Thomas • Tracie Williams • Steven Almánzar Cabrera • Fabrizia Costa • F. Vispo • Christopher Xavier Lozano • Hiroshi Katsumata • Gordon Baldwin • Eros Hoagland • Jeffrey Jacobson • Gina Paterno • Douniaux Valerie • Noriko Hayashi • Tadashi Fujita • Cornelia Stach • Rie Hayashi • Henry Jacobson • Sjors Swierstra • Joan Rosselle • Branden Eastwood • Eric Damon Walters • Pierre Albert Winter • Pablo Delano • Magnus Fun Inc. • C. Pertwee • Kazunori Yakuwa